Vietnam

EVERGREEN is an imprint of Benedikt Taschen Verlag GmbH

© for this edition: 1998 Benedikt Taschen Verlag GmbH
Hohenzollernring 53, D–50672 Köln
© 1997 Editions du Chêne – Hachette Livre – Le Viêt-nam
Under the direction of Michel Buntz – Hoa Qui Photographic Agency
Editor: Corinne Fossey
Maps and illustrations: Jean-Michel Kirsch
Text: Marc Rousseau
Photographs: Philippe Body and Jean-Léo Dugast
Cover: Angelika Taschen, Cologne
Translated by Phil Goddard
In association with First Edition Translations Ltd, Cambridge
Realization of the English edition by First Edition Translations Ltd, Cambridge

Printed in Italy
ISBN 3-8228-7758-1

VIETNAM

Text MARC ROUSSEAU

Photographs PHILIPPE BODY AND JEAN-LÉO DUGAST

EVERGREEN

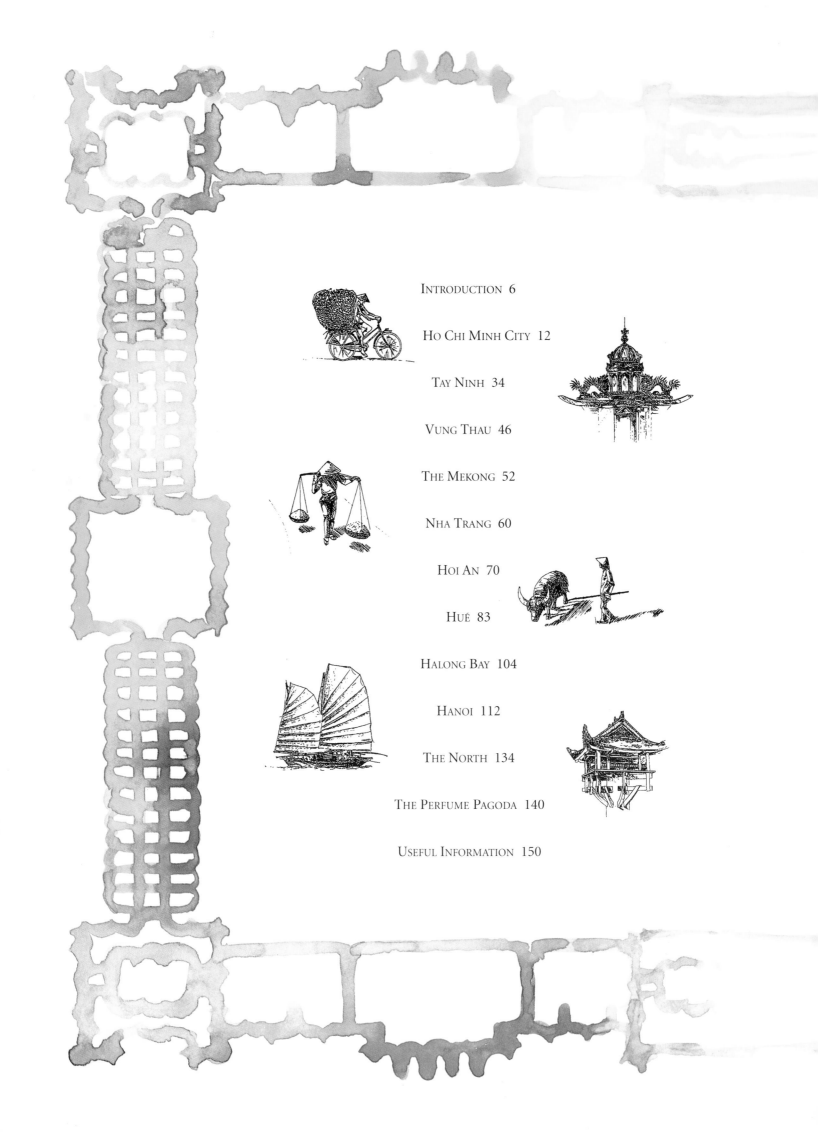

Mention the name Vietnam, and for almost three decades, from 1945 to 1975, most people thought of war. In Europe no less than in the US the image of this South-East Asian country was dominated by the Vietnam War – not least thanks to American films such as "Platoon" and "Apocalypse Now". But this war was just one in a long line of invasions and struggles for liberation that have punctuated Vietnam's age-old history.

Today the Vietnamese are fond of saying: "Vietnam is a country, not a war." Almost 60% of the people were born after the Vietnam War, and the ugly images of the war have long since been eclipsed by the beauty of the country, with its seemingly endless coastline, ravishing beaches and green paddy fields. Rice remains the most important staple, cultivated as early as 3000 years ago, initially in the Red River Delta, where the settlement of Vietnam began.

In 111 BC the delta was conquered by the Chinese, ushering in a strained relationship between the two peoples that lasts to this day. During their 1000-year overlordship the Chinese left an indelible mark especially on northern Vietnamese culture, introducing Confucianism and Taoism. Central and southern Vietnam, by contrast, were dominated by Indian influences. Following the end of Chinese rule in 939 AD, a now independent Vietnam revolved around three political centres: Tonkin with its capital Hanoi in the north, Annam with its capital Hué in the centre, and Cochin-China with its capital Saigon in the south. Independence also marked the beginning of Vietnam's dynasties. Once the attacking Mongols were beaten off (13th century) and renewed attention from the Chinese was rebuffed (15th century), the country came into its own, and the centuries following are considered Vietnam's cultural heyday.

From the 16th century onwards, when the south began to develop its own identity, tension arose between the peoples of the north and south. In the 17th and 18th centuries Vietnam split into two rival princedoms, the north being ruled by the Trinh dynasty, the south by the Nguyen dynasty. For more than 200 years (1593-1802) the border between the two parts was not crossed except by armies.

National reunification, when it came in 1802, was similarly brought about by military means and was accepted by the north only grudgingly, because the new ruler, Nguyen Anh, hailed from the south. Nguyen Anh proclaimed himself Emperor Ga Long and made Hué the new capital of united Vietnam. The magnificent imperial tombs of this dynasty, which ruled until 1945, can be seen around Hué, although the imperial residence in Hué, modelled on the "Forbidden City" in Peking, fell victim to the Vietnam War.

In Hanoi, Hué, Ho Chi Min City (formerly Saigon) and many other towns, numerous European-style houses and churches can be seen. Often slightly dilapidated, they are a legacy of Vietnam's colonial rulers. The history of Vietnamese-European relations began in 1516, when Portuguese sailors landed at Danang. They were quickly followed by Catholic missionaries, one of whom made a lasting contribution to Vietnamese culture – the French Jesuit Alexandre de Rhodes (1591-1660) established written Vietnamese, based on the Roman alphabet. In the 19th century renewed European interest in gaining access to China for trade purposes led to the colonization of Vietnam. France intervened in 1858, and by 1887 had merged Vietnam, Laos and Cambodia in the French Indo-Chinese union. The imperial family continued to exist, but was effectively powerless.

The Japanese, who in June 1940 had made Vietnam a kind of protectorate, released the country into independence on 9 March 1945. Two days later the Annamite emperor Bao Die revoked the protectorate treaty with France, meaning that only Cochin-China now remained under foreign rule.

On 2 September 1945 Ho Chi Minh proclaimed the Democratic Republic of Vietnam. Initially, in March 1946, France recognized the new republic, but then, during the First Indochina War (1946-54), sought to reverse developments, among other things installing a rival government in the south. In the wake of France's defeat in 1954, the 17th parallel was laid down at the Indochina conference in Geneva as the border between North and South, establishing the basis for the separate development of the two parts of the country.

In the north Ho Chi Minh, backed by the Soviet Union and the People's Republic of China, made a new beginning along Marxist-Leninist lines, while in the south France was replaced by the USA as the power factor. In 1963 the US-backed South Vietnamese anti-Communist Ngo Dinh Diem fell, precipitating a series of coups – the result of armed clashes within South Vietnam in the Second Indochina War (1964-1975), which went down in history as the Vietnam War. The massive support given by the Communist north to the Vietcong (the South Vietnamese freedom movement) caused the Americans to step up their military aid until in the end almost half a million US soldiers were stationed in South Vietnam. Increasingly the USA's military action affected the civilian population, provoking international protest.

Peace talks started in 1968 led to a ceasefire agreement in 1973 and marked the beginning of the withdrawal of US troops. In 1975 the North Vietnamese army overran the south, reuniting Vietnam under Communism. The upshot was an exodus of the population – about one million "boat people" took their lamentable chance on the open sea.

If during the war the leaders in Hanoi had understood how to exploit their position between the Soviet Union and China to their advantage, after the war they sided with the Soviet Union against China. At new year 1978/79 Vietnamese troops marched into Cambodia, prompting China, which politically was on Cambodia's side, to cross the Vietnamese border mid-February 1979, initiating the so-called Third Indochina War (1979-1989), which ended in the autumn of 1989 with Vietnam withdrawing from Cambodia.

In 1989 the eastern bloc countries, Vietnam's allies, collapsed, and the country began opening up to the West. The constitution was overhauled in 1992, and finally peace returned to the land between the Dragon Mountains in the north and the Mekong Delta in the south. Now millions of tourists visit the country, and the Vietnamese, despite their painful history, have remained a hospitable people, happy to share the beauty of their homeland with visitors.

Tatjana Flade

The Ben Nghe canal links the markets of Cholon (the Chinese district of Ho Chi Minh City) with the Saigon River and the city's port. Small boats ply the canal, carrying wares of every description. A boat trip along the canal provides a different perspective on Cholon, with its shops on stilts, its constant activity, and its extraordinary combination of colours, sounds, and smells.

Arriving in a strange city in an unknown country, after an overnight plane journey lasting many hours, always fills me with a mixture of shock and apprehension. It is rather like meeting someone on a first date.

Will I recognize her, given that I have only ever seen a photograph of her? Will she be taller, slimmer; will she have the same luminous smile that I imagine her having? Did the photograph, with its rather stiff, formal pose, really do justice to her? What will her perfume be like? Every city has its own distinctive smell. I know I could instantly recognize Istanbul or Bombay with my eyes closed, simply by inhaling the evening air.

The cabin door opens, and the dry and stuffy atmosphere of the aircraft is immediately replaced by humid heat and unfamiliar sounds. Standing at the top of the steps, I meet my first real live Vietnamese woman, from Ho Chi Minh City, wearing a long uniform dress of white satin. Is her beaming smile directed solely at me, or are all the other two hundred passengers graced with the same welcome? Surely not.

Above: Integrated transport at its best: buses are used for longer journeys, followed by a short hop on a bicycle.

Opposite: The whole of Ho Chi Minh City is one huge open-air market, where everything can be bought and sold. Everyone in Vietnam, from the farmers of the Mekong Delta to the shop owners in the big cities, seems to have a remarkable nose for business.

As the taxi honks its way through the rush-hour traffic, I open the window in an attempt to get used to the humid heat, and breathe in the atmosphere of the city, a hot wind still laden with the fragrance of the recent monsoon rain. I had better start getting used to the noise, too: the buzzing of millions of mopeds and motorcycles, and the ceaseless hooting of car horns.

At first sight, it looks like complete gridlock; but no, this is just the city going about its daily business, and there is order amid the apparent chaos. We turn off round a little square and into a dark side street with crumbling pavements, and here come the first images of the real Vietnam: red lanterns; a brief glimpse of an altar swathed in clouds of incense; an old woman staggering along under the weight of a huge wicker basket; stalls selling fruit, flowers, and hot food; children crowded into rickshaws; stunningly beautiful girls wearing white cotton gloves and the long pastel-coloured dresses known as *ao dais*, and riding huge black bicycles.

The city still does not seem to have made up its mind what to call itself. The taxi driver talks about Saigon, but when I arrive at the

A flower vendor thinks nothing of transporting her entire stock to market on the back of her bicycle. Nothing is too big or bulky to be transported in this way.

hotel, the receptionist says: "Welcome to Ho Chi Minh City." This is the city of Uncle Ho, who founded the Vietnamese Communist Party and was president of North Vietnam until his death in 1969. Today, many people refer to it by its former name of Saigon, though I found out much later that this is simply the name of one of its districts, District Number 1. It is no easy task to change the name of a city when it has such great symbolic resonance. Its official name is Ho Chi Minh City, and this is the name you will see on road signs and rail and air tickets, and in official guidebooks. Go to the ticket counter at the station and ask for a ticket to Saigon, and you will promptly be given a piece of cardboard marked "Ho Chi Minh City".

In the past, the name you called it by was an indicator of your political leanings. Nowadays the two names exist side by side, though no-one in any kind of official position will call it anything other than Ho Chi Minh City, often abbreviated to HCMC.

Perhaps the best rule of thumb you can follow as a foreigner is always to call it by its official name. It is impossible to lay down

A banana seller wheeling her stall through Ben Thanh market, one of the biggest and most lively markets in Cholon.

general rules, since there always seem to be exceptions. For example, the tag on my suitcase said SGN, which is the international airport code for Ho Chi Minh City. In some ways, this constant ambiguity is a metaphor for the enigma that is Indochina. Everything here has two faces, the official one and the hidden one, and any visit to Vietnam involves walking a tightrope between these two co-existing and sometimes conflicting realities. Sometimes this makes the trip even more enjoyable; at other times it can be incredibly frustrating – depending on what mood you happen to be in at the time. There is no single, fixed truth, and there are always at least two different ways of interpreting everything you see and experience, like one of those holograms that change colour or perspective depending on the angle from which you look at them. Saigon was the capital of South Vietnam until it was captured by the advancing North Vietnamese forces in 1975. Nowadays it has a distinctly rebellious, decadent streak, contrasting starkly with Hanoi's puritanical air. Thirty years of independence have given Ho Chi Minh City a soul that it lacked before.

*A*bove and opposite: There are believed to be over two million bicycles, mopeds, and
motorbikes in Ho Chi Minh City; vehicles with two wheels outnumber those with four.
Below: A cyclo, or pedicab, transports children home from school.

• Vietnamese names •

Most Vietnamese have three names; the more educated people may have up to five,
while peasants sometimes have only one. The first is the family or clan name, which
is handed down from the father to his children. There are only about a dozen family
names in the entire country. The middle name is a quality or virtue that the parents
hope the child will have. For example, the boy's name Van means success, while
the girl's name Thi signifies fertility. Forenames, which in fact come last, may be chosen from a great
variety of alternatives: Lien means lotus, Lan means orchid, Hong means rose, Ngoc means jade, Thuy
means pearl, and so on. Some people, particularly in rural areas, may have a nickname: Mao means
cat, and is a name given to those born in the year of the cat, while Hai means youngest. Catholics
give themselves a Christian first name, while educated people may have a pen-name or pseudonym.

*B*urning a bunch of incense sticks
in Cholon's Tan Son Hai Pagoda
to bring good fortune.

This being the beginning of my trip, I decided I ought to obtain some sort of blessing to make sure that no ill-fortune befell me. My guide said this was no problem. His name was Pham Van Dong, and he told me that his middle name meant "success", which I took to be a good omen in itself. All we had to do, he assured me, was to visit one of the city's many pagodas and make suitable offerings.

I had to be honest with Dong, and I admitted I was not a Buddhist. "Don't worry about that", he told me. "There's a first time for everything, and it can't do any harm. Anyway, I was thinking of going there myself, so you might as well come with me. You'll find that people are very tolerant here. Provided you play by the rules, it's perfectly all right for a foreigner to come along and ask for divine blessing."

The next problem was which pagoda to visit. We were spoilt for choice. There was Giac Lam, one of the most ancient, where a dozen monks still lived; there was Giac Ven; or we could go to the Jade Emperor Pagoda, one of the most spectacular in the city, which was home to many divinities and statues of heroic figures.

*H*uge bunches of purple incense sticks on sale to worshippers at the entrance to the double pagoda of Giac Lam, in Ho Chi Minh City. The sticks are placed in a cup full of sand. Their fragrant smoke symbolizes spiritual elevation, prayer rising to the gods and the souls of the dead, and purification of the living.

Alternatively, we could go to Cholon, the city's huge Chinese district. Here, we could choose between An Quang, which was a rebel stronghold in the Vietnam war; Chua Be Chua, dedicated to the goddess of fertility; Thien Hau, the pagoda of the sea goddess; and Phuoc An Hoi Quam, with its beautiful porcelain miniatures. Eventually, we chose the nearest. We strode in to the inner courtyard, which was surrounded by open-fronted, colonnaded buildings. At the far end were the altars, with hundreds of incense sticks burning in front of them. We walked once around the main altar from west to east in the direction of the earth's rotation. Then we followed the example of every other visitor by buying a large coil of incense. Some of these are up to 50 centimetres (20 in) in diameter. We lit this, and asked the monk on duty to attach it to the ceiling using the hook provided for the purpose. Now, for as long as it went on burning – and a generous donation ensured that it would do so for a long time – no evil would befall us on our journey. Our coil, which had now flopped down to form a cone shape, would be watching over us.

Incense originally comes from Yemen and the Sultanate of Oman. There are around three hundred different kinds of trees which can be used, but those which produce the purest incense can be found only in this region. The incense is harvested in the form of a gum or resin. This resin is dried, broken up into small pieces, and then pounded and crushed to make a very fine white, brown, or mustard-coloured flammable powder, depending on the quality required. When burned, the powder gives off thick white smoke and a distinctive aroma. It can be used either as it is, or perfumed with rose, sandalwood, jasmine, or a variety of other substances. Although in the west it is usually sold packed round a fine wooden stick that is used as a taper, elsewhere it is most often made into cones or small blocks, or is stuck onto coils of very fine rattan or other material. Incense has existed since very ancient times, and has always been associated with purification ceremonies. It was, and still is, used by the majority of religions. When the three wise men brought incense as a gift to the infant Christ, they did so because it was a symbol of priesthood.

Long, spiral-shaped cones of
incense hang from the ceiling of
a pagoda, burning for days and
sometimes weeks. As long as they go
on smoking, the donor will be
protected from ill-fortune.

Each of the monks in Giac Lam Pagoda has his own bowl, which is used for both collecting alms and making offerings. Any Buddhist can become a monk. Some do so for a week or a month, others for years or even a lifetime.

Superstition still plays an important part in everyday Vietnamese life, and people often consult horoscopes, soothsayers, and geomancers. Nobody would even dream of setting up a company, opening a restaurant, or building a house without making use of their services. If you think a door is rather oddly positioned, this is probably because it will allow benevolent spirits to enter the building more easily.

Ancestor worship is often believed to be a Confucian practice, but in fact it is much more ancient. All Vietnamese engage in it, be they Christians, Buddhists, Taoists, or Caodaists. Some households pay homage to their ancestors on a daily basis; others only on the anniversary of their deaths. The spirits continue to watch over and protect their descendants, and it would be very risky not to show respect by making offerings of flowers, fruit, and banknotes.

Every traditional Vietnamese house has its own altar, on which commemorative tablets are placed, often taking the form of simple plaques bearing the names of the dead, with incense sticks or oil lamps burning in front of them.

*A*lthough Vietnam has a number of different religions, there are many similarities between their various iconographies. Christians in Van Gam Church use plaques (left) and urns (below) to commemorate the dead.

*L*ikewise, in the Buddhist pagoda of Vin Liem, worshippers place plaques on the walls as a sign of their faith, hope, and gratitude to the gods.

*T*et, or the Vietnamese new year, is one of the country's most picturesque, colourful, and noisy festivals. A dragon made of brightly painted wood, cardboard, and papier mâché dances through the streets, symbolizing the exuberance of new life and the arrival of spring.

The most important Vietnamese festival is Tet, held during the first week of the first lunar month, in late January or early February. This is a celebration of the new year. Everyone dons new clothes, pays their debts, and gives their house a thorough spring-cleaning. The main ceremony takes place on the first evening of Tet, when families prepare a symbolic meal for the dead and then hold a party. Another festival that is also linked to the worship of the dead takes place at the beginning of April, when people make offerings of paper money and flowers to their ancestors.

The summer solstice festival is a reminder that, although nature is at the height of its powers, the decline that leads inexorably into autumn and winter has begun. It is at this time of abundance that people honour the spirits of the dead and the ghosts and spectres of winter. Another festival, Wandering Souls' Day, takes place at the end of summer, and commemorates those who have died and been forgotten. Finally, the Mid-Autumn festival, held when the moon reaches its apogee, is a time for making lanterns, shaped like fish, junks, or buffalo, and moon cakes, made using lotus flowers and egg yolks.

Canary-yellow and pink silk screens are left out to dry in the street, before being stretched on lacquered bamboo frames. These fragile objects will be used as decorations during the Tet festival.

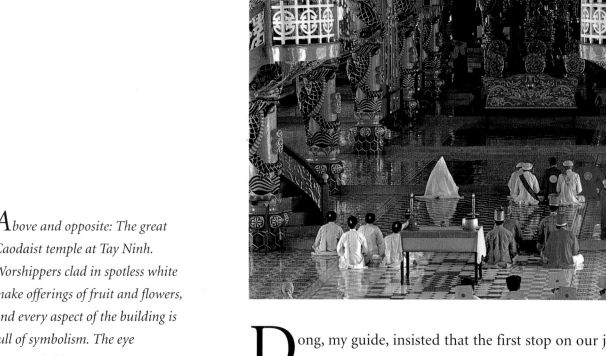

Above and opposite: The great Caodaist temple at Tay Ninh. Worshippers clad in spotless white make offerings of fruit and flowers, and every aspect of the building is full of symbolism. The eye surrounded by rays represents knowledge, awareness, and the spirit shining its light on the world.

Dong, my guide, insisted that the first stop on our journey should be the small town of Tay Ninh – so small, in fact, that it barely featured on my maps. Why there? "Well, it's a bit like Rome is to Catholics; it's the centre of our religion", he explained. "But I thought you were a Buddhist!" I exclaimed. "Surely that was a Buddhist pagoda we went to in Ho Chi Minh City?" "That's right", Dong replied. "I practise Caodaism, which is a bit of an unusual religion." I soon found out that "unusual" was an understatement. Established early this century, Caodaism is a synthesis of eastern and western faiths, describing itself as a "third alliance" between God and man. It combines Buddhism, Taoism, Confucianism, Islam, and Catholicism, with a single God who is assisted by an earth goddess and an extraordinary array of saints including Jesus, Moses, Mohammed, Descartes, Lenin, Louis Pasteur, Shakespeare, Julius Caesar, and Joan of Arc.

By the 1950s, one in five South Vietnamese practised this religion, which imposes a strict ban on killing and teaches that mankind is essentially good. During the war Caodaists refused to fight, and at

the beginning of the conflict they opposed the Vietcong. After reunification they were persecuted. However, the religion now has some four hundred temples and an estimated two million adherents, concentrated in the centre and south of the country, particularly in the Mekong Delta.

Cao Dai is one of Vietnam's strangest religions. It is also a recent one, having only been recognized as such since 1925. Its founder, Ngo Minh Chieu, sometimes called Ngo Van Chieu, was born in 1878. He was a civil servant responsible for administering the tropical island of Phu Quoc, near the Cambodian border in the far south of the country. Chieu was a mystic and a strong believer in spiritualism, and was fascinated by western and oriental religions. He was also greatly attracted to humanism, and was influenced by the advances made by late nineteenth-century science. The religion he created was based on Buddhism, but embodied aspects of all these tendencies; hence its belief in "saints". Around 1919, Chieu claimed to have received divine revelations at a series of spiritualist séances, mainly from a figure he called Cao Dai, which means

Caodaism describes itself as the third alliance between God and man. It believes in a single God, who is associated with an earth goddess, and combines elements of many different religions. Figures of Confucius and mythological dragons both have their place beneath the dome of the Caodaist temple at Tay Ninh.

The Caodaists worship many different spirits, including Mohammed, Louis Pasteur, Lenin, Jesus, Descartes, and Moses.

literally "High Tower" or "Supreme Palace", in other words, God. He developed a doctrine for his new religion, and gained many followers. By the time Caodaism was officially recognized in 1925, it had some 25,000 adherents, recruited mainly from the civil service and the colonial administration, with which it developed close links. The religion is based on the same principle as Buddhism: the quest for a way of escaping the endless cycle of reincarnation. If they are to achieve this, Caodaists must be fundamentally good; they may not kill, steal, or tell lies, and must lead pure, if not totally ascetic, lives. But Caodaism also borrows from the two other great religions of Vietnam, Taoism and Confucianism, as well as from traditional indigenous beliefs such as animism and ancestor worship. It has many sympathies with Christianity, and shares the same belief in a single God. As part of its eclectic approach, it has elevated major eastern and western figures to the status of saints. Apart from the figures we have already mentioned, the list includes Victor Hugo, who, like Ngo Minh Chieu, was himself a spiritualist.

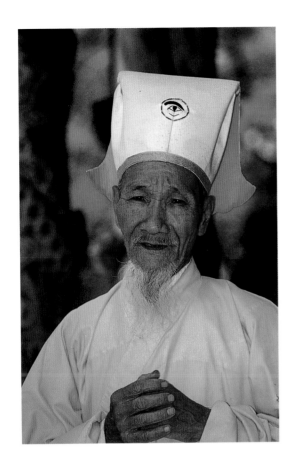

*T*his page and overleaf:
Worshippers at the Caodai temple.
The man in the yellow robe is a
senior Buddhist dignitary, while the
younger one in red is a Confucianist
initiate. Both wear the eye that
symbolizes universal knowledge.
Ordinary worshippers, wearing
white, are watched over by a
benevolent dragon.

Caodaist women on their way to the temple.

The theology of Caodaism is therefore highly complex. Although it has only one God, its belief in the principles of Yin and Yang has led it to adopt a second, female deity, the earth goddess, with God representing the masculine principle. Adherents also believe that although the first divine revelation was given to Lao Tzu, parts of it were also granted at different times and in different places to Buddha, Mohammed, Confucius, Jesus, and Moses. Ngo Minh Chieu himself received the Final Revelation.

Caodaists are vegetarians. They have a mission to convert other people, and practise meditation either alone or in public ceremonies. The most visible aspect of the religion is its offerings of flowers and fruit. The clergy are unpaid, and only priests make a vow of celibacy.

Women theoretically enjoy equality with men, but only men may become senior members of the clergy, and male priests are in the place of honour during acts of worship, which are conducted four times a day: at 6 am, midday, 6 pm, and midnight.

Foreigners are generally welcome in Caodaist temples, which are

built on nine levels symbolizing the nine stages of supreme wisdom, and photography is allowed during some ceremonies. Some aspects of these rites are closely linked to spiritualism. Examples are automatic writing by a medium and the receipt of divine messages, which are sealed in a white envelope hanging above the altar. These communications with the spirits are generally in Vietnamese, though they may also take place in English, French, or even Chinese. The Caodaists supported the Japanese during the Second World War and the French during the colonial period, and opposed the Vietcong in the Vietnam war.

The tomb of a senior Caodaist dignitary, the equivalent of a cardinal, at Tay Ninh. It is decorated with the figures of familiar animal deities and dragons, along with the universal wheel of the Hindus and Solomon's seal.

*B*ringing in the catch at Vung Thau, a town with a thriving fishing industry. Like fishing boats the world over, each of the sampans is marked with an eye to ward off evil.

The fishing port of Vung Thau, known as Cap Saint-Jacques during the French occupation, is still a favourite destination for excursions from Ho Chi Minh City. Although it is 120 kilometres (75 miles) from the southern capital, it is the closest beach to the city. Vung Thau's former colonial villas have been converted into boarding houses for visitors lured there by its warm tropical waters and extensive beaches, the biggest of which is 8 kilometres (5 miles) long.

Neither Dong nor I was particularly enamoured of beaches. Instead, we went to see the town's fine pagodas; its lighthouse, which has a spectacular view; its giant statue of Christ; and the Villa Blanche, which was the home of Paul Doumer, the French governor-general at the turn of the century. The elderly caretaker told us that the villa was named after Doumer's daughter, Blanche. This architectural gem was used to imprison Emperor Thanh Thai after he was deposed by the French in 1907 for conspiring against them, and was the residence of Nguyen Van Thieu, the president of South Vietnam from 1967 to 1975.

*A*bove: A woman rows her boat
across the Mekong Delta at Cantho.
Opposite: The floating market at Cai
Rang sells fruit and vegetables from
all over the delta.
Overleaf: Sunset over the Mekong
Delta. The Mekong is the most
important of Vietnam's rivers, and
its delta forms a tangled web of
channels and canals stretching from
the Cambodian border to the South
China Sea.

*W*e took the ferry round the southern tip of the Mekong
Delta to the town of Rach Gia. Sediment from the River
of the Nine Dragons, as the Vietnamese call the Mekong, has created a huge, flat alluvial plain in southern Vietnam, divided by the
many branches of the river. The Plain of Rushes extends to the
north of the delta; to the south is the vast Ca Mau peninsula.

The Mekong Delta is often compared to the Red River Delta, in
northern Vietnam, but it is nearly three times as large, at around
50,000 square kilometres (20,000 square miles). As well as the
branches of the river, there are also many canals, and it can be quite
hard to work out what is natural and what is man-made. Altogether,
there are perhaps 5,000 kilometres (3,000 miles) of waterways, and
the region is never more than about 2 metres (7 ft) above the level
of the water. Here, the tide retreats up to 300 kilometres (190 miles)
inland, and in some places the shore of the South China Sea is silt-
ing up at a rate of 80 metres (250 ft) a year, transporting the fertile
soils of China, Laos, and Cambodia southwards and patiently creat-
ing new marshlands that can be used for planting rice.

*A*bove: Woman selling peppers in
Cai Rang.
Top left, above right, and opposite:
At Cantho's floating market, the
canals are the streets and the boats
double as market stalls.

The population structure of the Mekong Delta has been influenced by its proximity to Cambodia. Although the people are predominantly Vietnamese, there are also many Khmers. It was in the delta that the rivalry between the two countries began, since the Cambodians saw it as a natural extension of their own country, while the Vietnamese regarded it as an essential component of theirs. Since the delta gets both its water and its soil from Cambodia, it has sometimes been called *Kampuchea Krom*, or Downstream Cambodia.

The French deliberately drew a clear dividing line between Cochin-China, or southern Vietnam; Annam, the central region; and Tonkin, in the north. Cochin-China was originally colonized by Vietnamese from Hué during the Nguyen empire, before being occupied by the French. In the mid-nineteenth century only half the

In the Mekong Delta much of life revolves around fishing.
Opposite: The laborious task of repairing the nets is regarded as women's work.
Above: This boatman in My Tho, in the Mekong Delta, earns his living ferrying people
across the Bao Dinh canal.

• The art of eating •

Meals usually consist of a bowl of rice with meat, fish, or vegetables on top, often with a sauce poured over it. The rice is topped up from a bowl in the centre of the table, using a spoon.

Holding your chopsticks two-thirds of the way along rather than in the middle, raise your bowl to your mouth, and lift the food into your mouth with the chopsticks held almost vertically.

When you have had enough, place the chopsticks flat across the bowl. Never stand them in the rice, since this resembles the incense sticks planted in containers and used in ancestor worship, and would therefore be associated with death.

Above and opposite: Cochin-China's famous conical hats are made by the women, using dried and woven palm leaves.

population was Vietnamese, and it was not until the French colonial period, when Norodom was crowned emperor in Ho Chi Minh City, that Chinese and Vietnamese immigrants moved into the delta.

It was more by accident than by design that the Mekong Delta became Vietnamese. For a long time, it was little known to foreigners, and travellers had to contend with bad roads and numerous ferry crossings. To make matters worse, there was no cool season to provide relief from the very hot and humid climate.

There is little in the way of dramatic landscape here, except on the island of Phu Quoc in the Gulf of Thailand. This is closer to Cambodia than to Vietnam, and the Cambodians are therefore claiming sovereignty over it. Phu Quoc is a steep-sided, verdant island with immaculate beaches and azure waters, and will probably end up as a major tourist resort. But for the time being at least, the coves are deserted, and the villagers are content to cultivate pepper, copra, and coconuts, and to make *nuoc mam*, the ubiquitous fish sauce.

The landscape of the delta is one of pagodas, temples, tombs, for-
tifications, islands large and small, and fishing ports. Its endless
rice-fields make it extraordinarily green, and everywhere you look
you will see typically Vietnamese scenes: people in conical rice-
straw hats pricking out rice seedlings and ploughing the fields; buffaloes being ridden by children or asleep with the water up to their
snouts; fishermen standing on tiny islets hauling in their nets; skeins
of ducks winging their way across the sky; sheaves of rice-straw
laid out to dry beside the road; junks with mud-brown sails pick-
ing their way through the reeds in the distance. These scenes are
played out against a dazzling, mirror-like and seemingly endless
expanse of water, for this is neither land, nor river, nor sea – it is the
Mekong Delta.

Overleaf: Salt being transported in traditional Vietnamese style at the Phan Thiet salt pans in Cochin-China, on the coast of the South China Sea.

*A*bove and opposite: *The white sandy beaches of Muy Nai, on the Gulf of Thailand.*
This region, very near the Cambodian border and overlooking the island of Phu Quoc,
is renowned for its seafood, black pepper, and turtles.

• Vietnamese cuisine •

Vietnamese food is distinguished by its very great variety of ingredients and ways of preparing them. It is also quite light, since it uses little fat and plenty of vegetables and herbs. Unlike Chinese food, it makes little use of soy sauce; instead, most dishes are served with a strongly flavoured sauce called *nuoc mam*, made from fish fermented in salt.

Meat is expensive and relatively little used, whereas fish is very abundant in the lakes, rivers, and seas of Vietnam. Rice is the staple diet, the Vietnamese equivalent of bread, though one legacy of French rule is excellent baguettes.

Apart from a very wide variety of fruit juices, the most popular drinks are green tea, beer, and rice wine.

We were lucky in Nha Trang, for this was late June and the dry season runs from mid-June to mid-September, the opposite to Ho Chi Minh City's. My guide for this section of the journey, the charming Thuy Chau, told me that even in the autumn months, which were the wettest, much of the rain fell very early in the morning, around sunrise.

I took an immediate liking to this photogenic seaside resort, with its translucent waters, coral-sand beaches, tropical fish, and superb diving and snorkelling. The climate is ideal nearly all year round, and the sheltered bay means that the sea is safe to swim in. As you might expect from a fishing port that has Vietnam's biggest fleet of junks, sampans, and trawlers, fish and seafood are on the menu everywhere here: tuna, cuttlefish, octopus, squid, bonito, lobster, crayfish, and shellfish of all shapes and sizes. Nha Trang is the fish capital of Vietnam, and the industry has helped to make the city, and the province of the same name, among the most affluent in the country. Other industries include coffee, sesame, cashew nuts, and sea salt, but this is also the region with the greatest tourist potential.

The Vietnamese are very much aware of this, and dream of turning Nha Trang and Bamboo Island, just offshore, into the Phuket of the South China Sea.

The beach resort of Nha Trang on the South China Sea, with its unusually transparent turquoise waters, is gradually opening up to foreign tourists. However, fishing is still one of its main activities, and many fishermen live in villages on stilts on the offshore islands.

All forms of fishing are practised at Nha Trang, and the region is rich in fish and shellfish, including mackerel, tuna, scallops, lobsters, crayfish, and cuttlefish. Top: Collecting crabs' eggs on the beach. Overleaf: Fishermen in Hoi An taking a rest from their labours.

To see Nha Trang at its best, you need to go north out of town and cross the Xom Bong Bridge to the Hon Chong promontory, which overlooks the islands of the bay. It was here that Thuy Chau (whose name means "pearl of water") told me the story of how the islands and Fairy Mountain came to be there.

"See that handprint on that great big rock? Well, once upon a time, there was a giant who spied on a fairy while she was bathing. They fell in love and began living together, but the gods were very jealous, and sent the giant into exile. The fairy thought he would never return, and died of grief. That mountain is her dead body stretched out on the ground; that's her head over there; those are her breasts, and those are her bent knees. The giant did eventually come back, and when he saw that the fairy was dead, he collapsed beside her, leaving his handprint on her body."

This page: A heavily laden boat on the Thu Bon River in Hoi An, Annam.

Opposite: Fish are abundant in the seas around Vietnam, and are a staple part of the country's diet. Small-scale fishing is practised everywhere along the coast.

A short distance along the coast to the north-east is the former city of Fai Fo, now known as Hoi An. In ancient times, it was the main port of the Kingdom of Champa, and more recently, until the nineteenth century, it was a major staging-post on the silk route, visited by merchant vessels from all over Europe and Asia. For four hundred years, merchants from China and Japan built warehouses here, which also doubled as communal living-quarters. A number of these elegant buildings have been remarkably well preserved, giving the town a slightly faded charm. Many of them are still in use, with their ground floors serving as shops, and some have retained the painted wooden shelves whose design has remained unchanged since medieval times. They have brick walls and bright red or emerald-green Chinese-style glazed tile roofs. Through these, you can see beams made from the hard, black wood of the jackfruit tree. Strolling through town is like taking a walk back through history, even though the merchandise nowadays tends to be carried on tri-cycles rather than by coolies, and there are tangles of electrical cables on the fronts of buildings that have seen better days. Around

a hundred of these old buildings are still intact, some dating from the fifteenth century and others from the French colonial period, when Hoi An became an important administrative centre. The government has decided to preserve the town's rich architectural heritage by contributing towards their maintenance, and has begun a restoration programme for those that are most dilapidated.

Another distinctive feature of Hoi An is the communal assembly halls, each built by immigrants from a particular region of China such as Guangdong, Fukien, Chaozhao, and Hainan, the large island to the west of Hong Kong. The Chinese All-Community Assembly Hall, or Chua Ba, dates from 1773 and was built for merchants from other provinces who could not afford their own.

All of Hoi An's historic houses have more or less intact interiors, complete with altars, engravings, statues, commemorative plaques, model boats, magnificent doors decorated with wooden eyes bearing the Yin and Yang symbol to protect the occupants against bad luck, and murals depicting everyday life at the time when Hoi An was a major trading port.

*L*eft: *Buffalo are used to plough the soil, carry sheaves of straw and bags of rice,
and sometimes even as a form of transport for humans.*
*Above: Yokes can be used to carry just about everything. The loads on either side have to
be carefully balanced, and this results in a distinctive dancing gait.*

• Language and politeness •

Vietnamese is a complex language, of various origins. It is written using the Roman alphabet, with accents over the vowels to indicate tones, which are used to distinguish between different meanings of what would otherwise be the same word. Northern Vietnamese has six tones, while southern dialects have five. For example, the word *ma* may mean "horse", "cheek", "but", "ghost", or "tomb" depending on the intonation. In some cases, there are different words for the same concept depending on whether you are in the north or the south, and also on whether you are a man or a woman. In Hanoi, the word for "yes" is *ya*, but in Ho Chi Minh City it is *da*. There are various ways of saying hello: men use *anh* when speaking to an equal or a young man, *ong* as a sign of respect to an elderly man, and *ba* as the polite form when addressing a woman. A woman will say *co* to a girl, but *hi* to an old woman.

The ancient, very cosmopolitan city of Hoi An, on the Thu Bon River. Once a prosperous port on the silk route, it has now silted up.

One very distinctive landmark is the sixteenth-century Japanese covered bridge, built across the Thu Bon River as a symbolic link between the Japanese and Chinese quarters. The bridge is supposed to have been started in the year of the monkey and completed in the year of the dog. It is therefore guarded by two stone monkeys at the southern end and two watchful dogs on the northern side, where there is a miniature temple. According to legend, this was built to appease the dragon that causes earthquakes in the Hoi An region. The town has many other architectural treasures, including a number of private houses once owned by wealthy merchants. One is Tan Ky House, built in Chinese and Japanese style with a carved wooden atrium courtyard; another is Diep Dong Nguyen House, built by an apothecary in the last century and still lived in by his great-grandchildren. A surprising number of wells have survived despite the rising demand for mains drinking-water, and there are numerous pagodas that bear witness to the mix of cultures and peoples in Hoi An, including the fifteenth-century Chuc Than Pagoda, the Caodai Pagoda, and the Truong Family Chapel.

There is no point in seeking out the port, since it no longer exists. The Thu Bon River became silted up at the end of the last century, sounding the death knell of the old city, and it was supplanted by its great northern rival, Danang. But I still wanted a view of the town from the sea, to help me imagine the endless cavalcade of ships that had passed through here: merchant sailing ships, sampans, long Chinese ships with oars, junks, brigs, schooners, Hanseatic trading vessels, Flemish carracks, Spanish galleons, store ships, English coasters, frigates, corvettes. So we went to the fine sandy beach of Cua Dai, where we took a rather more modern ferry to the two neighbouring islands: Cam Kim, which still has its old naval shipyards, and Cham, famous for its swallow's-nest soup. Back in Hoi An, I noticed the rhythmic clacking of the cotton weavers, which is the heartbeat of the town today. Its former glories may be disappearing under accumulated layers of sand, but it is a living, breathing town nevertheless.

The town that took over Hoi An's role as it silted up from 1950 onwards was Tourane, now known as Danang. This is Vietnam's

Hoi An is a jumble of architectural styles: Vietnamese, Chinese, Japanese, and in this case French colonial.

This page: Many of the old merchants' houses in Hoi An have elaborately crafted doors.
Opposite: One of the wooden statues in Phuoc Kien Pagoda, Hoi An.
Overleaf: The main entrance to Phuoc Kien Pagoda, which combines Chinese and Japanese architecture.

fourth largest city, and was used as a base first by the American navy, until 1975, and then by the Soviets. It played an important part in the war, and the Americans were forced to flee before the city fell into Vietcong hands. The most dramatic episode in this débâcle remains indelibly etched in the memory of every inhabitant of Danang who was alive at the time. On 27 March 1975, two Boeing 727s tried to evacuate one thousand refugees. There was a pitched battle between those trying to get on board, and many people who failed to do so hung on to the undercarriage of the first aircraft as it took off amid a hail of shells. They could not hold on, and were filmed by cameras on the second aircraft as they fell to their deaths in the sea.

The Cham Museum in Danang is a must if you want to understand the extraordinary ancient civilization of the Champa kingdom. Built by the Ecole Française d'Extrême Orient in 1915, it houses several hundred important items from the main excavation sites, including lingams, altars, and statues of Shiva, Ganesh, Vishnu, and Brahma.

Opposite: Sugar cane is still harvested by hand, using machetes.
Above: After each harvest, the rice paddies are turned over using a buffalo-drawn plough.
Buffaloes are the only animals capable of working in the flooded fields.

• Vietnam and its animals •

Vietnam has a very rich and varied fauna, but like everywhere else in the world, some species are dying out. These are strictly protected. Millions of brilliantly coloured tropical fish inhabit the coral reefs, and in many places they can be seen with the aid of a snorkel and mask. Seals, dolphins, and sea turtles also live off the coast. The protected species include elephants, tigers, leopards, black and brown bears, rhinoceroses, and numerous species of primates including gibbons, macaques, and rhesus monkeys. There are almost no tapirs left, but the mountains are home to such exotic creatures as wild peacocks, flying squirrels, deer, and wild buffalo, while the marshes and some rivers are inhabited by crocodiles, tortoises, cobras, and pythons.

Tending the rice paddies is a back-breakingly laborious task.
After being harvested, the rice is tied up in bundles and left to dry on the banks of earth alongside the fields.

We continued our exploration of the Mandarin Road in Hué, the central point from where it heads off towards northern and southern Vietnam. Hué is the former imperial capital, a city of writers, poets, painters, and musicians. Its history is visible everywhere you look, in its ramparts, moats, palaces, pagodas, tombs, and watchtowers.

Until the eleventh century, Hué was one of the great cities of the Champa empire. Then it gradually reverted to the status of a citadel. In 1744, it became the capital of the Nguyen dynasty, which ruled Vietnam for centuries, and was known as Phu Xuan. It was then occupied by rebels during the Tay Son rebellion of the 1770s and 1780s. Later on, in 1802, the Nguyen emperors again took advantage of its excellent location and great symbolic importance, baptizing the city Hué and making it the capital of their empire. Gia Long, the first emperor, decided to build "the most beautiful city in all the known universe". The old royal city lies in a valley in the shadow of five mountains, which are believed to represent the five basic elements. To the north, the Cloud Pass protects it against

A woman in one of Hué's outdoor markets sells fruit, vegetable, and herb purées, cooked in banana leaves and tied up with palm fronds.

unwanted outsiders, while the Hué or Perfume River flows through the south of the city.

Hué is now a living, open-air museum, but it is still the cultural capital of Vietnam as well. It spans both sides of the river, and despite the severe destruction wrought by the war, the French quarter on the right bank is largely intact. Several large hotels have been built here since the tourists started coming back, and the Vy Da district, in particular, has benefited greatly. This is the artistic heart of Hué, a meeting-place for intellectuals, poets, painters, writers, and musicians. The Citadel, or old town, is on the left bank, surrounded by moats and ramparts.

We entered the Citadel from the south, via the Phu Xuan Bridge, which bears the former name of the city. Soon, we reached the walls of the Imperial Enclosure, by the Quang Duc Gate and the Flag Tower. The tower is guarded by nine enormous cannons, variously believed to represent the five elements and the four seasons or the Nguyen emperors who still watch over the city. Only the emperor could use the South Gate, which led straight to the Forbidden

Purple City. Ordinary people had to enter by the other three gates.
The Forbidden Purple City, along with its walls and its seven symbolic gates, each reserved for a particular purpose, is no more. This
priceless treasure of Vietnamese architecture was destroyed by the
Vietcong during the Tet offensive of 1968, and all that remains of
this magnificent royal residence are a few fading photographs.
Fortunately, many other architectural wonders have survived, including Thai Hoa Palace, with its eight red-lacquered columns and traditional roof decorated with dragons, which was the emperor's official
reception hall. Other relics of this era in Vietnam's history include
the Nine Dynastic Urns, huge nineteenth-century pieces each com-
memorating one of the Nguyen emperors; and the Imperial Museum,
a former mandarin's palace, which still retains its former grandeur.
Curiously, the monuments that have survived with the least damage are the magnificent imperial tombs just outside the city. At least
six of these have been remarkably well preserved, and their overall
structure gives an idea of the splendour of the city when the emperors were alive.

*O*verleaf:
Noodle-sellers in the little village
of Tam Quan in Annam.

Each of the mausoleums comprises an entrance pavilion, a temple with altars for the worship of the dead, and the great fortified imperial tomb itself. Each has an honour courtyard decorated with stone statues of elephants, civil and military mandarins (wearing square and round hats respectively), dragons, phoenixes, and horses. Finally, each has an artificial lake seeded with lotuses.

The Mandarin Road, which links Hué with Hanoi and Ho Chi Minh City, dates from the time of Gia Long, who reigned from 1802 to 1819 and was the first of the thirteen emperors of the Nguyen dynasty, which remained in power until 1945. Gia Long was aware of the need to create a stronger basis for his empire, and relied on the more conservative forces in Vietnam, including the Confucianists, for support. He began a huge programme of major public projects including ports, dykes, canals, roads, and fortresses.

Opposite: A timeless Vietnamese scene: a farmer planting rice, surrounded by a great expanse of water.
Above: A duck-farmer tending his protégés near Hué.

*A*bove, opposite, and overleaf: The tomb of Khai Dinh, the last but one emperor
of the Nguyen dynasty, in the ancient imperial city of Hué.
The building is decorated in an extraordinary mix of
Vietnamese, Chinese, and Hindu motifs.

• Ancestor worship •

Ancestor worship is often believed to be a Confucian practice, but in fact it is much more ancient. All Vietnamese engage in it to a greater or lesser extent, be they Christians, Buddhists, Taoists, or Caodaists.

Some households pay homage to their ancestors on a daily basis, others only on the anniversary of their deaths. The spirits continue to watch over and protect their descendants, and it would be very risky not to show respect by making offerings of flowers, fruit, and banknotes.

Every traditional Vietnamese house has its own altar on which commemorative tablets are placed, often taking the form of simple plaques bearing the names of the dead, with incense sticks or oil lamps burning in front of them.

This page and opposite: The tombs of the Nguyen dynasty of emperors, near Hué. All are built in the same format, with an entrance pavilion and an honour courtyard, guarded by statues of civil or military mandarins. The round hats of the statues shown here indicate that they are military figures.

Later, his son Minh Mang strengthened the influence of Confucianism and clamped down on Christianity, which was becoming increasingly widespread. He also made the mistake of increasing taxes and the use of forced labour, which were already so oppressive that the people had been bled dry. They rebelled, and the result was even greater oppression. The administration ground to a halt, and Minh Mang's successors proved to be even more conservative. But Hué, the capital of the dynasty, remained an extremely important centre for writers, painters, poets, and musicians, particularly in the first part of the nineteenth century. It was during this period that the greatest masterpieces of Vietnamese literature were written, including *Kim Van Kieu*, the great narrative poem by Nguyen Du (1765–1820).

But the French had their eyes on the empire, even before the time of Napoleon III. In 1885, just after the great emperor Tu Duc had died, and following lengthy fighting, they captured Hué and installed a puppet emperor. The dynasty continued until the Second World War, but it was only a shadow of the former glorious regime.

Overleaf: The glazed tiles and lacquered woodwork of the ceremonial balcony above the Noontime Gate, which stands at the entrance to the imperial city in Hué.

*A*bove: *Detail from one of the Nine Dynastic Urns, in Hué's Forbidden City.*
Opposite: The altar in the tomb of Dong Khanh, the puppet emperor
installed by the French, who ruled from 1886 to 1888.

• Lacquer •

Vietnam is well known for its traditional lacquered objects. The basic ingredient of lacquer is the resin of the sumac, or lacquer tree, known as the *cay son* in Vietnamese.

This resin, similar to that of the hevea rubber tree, is left to dry for at least two days. Depending on the temperature, the drying time, and any plant colorants that are added, it becomes black, brown, beige, or scarlet.

Thin layers of lacquer are then applied to an object made of wood (often teak) or papier mâché. A good lacquer will require at least eleven layers. Each one has to be left to dry for around a week, and is then sanded and polished before the next coat is added.

The Thien Mu, or Fairy Woman Pagoda, stands on a hill overlooking the Perfume River, near Hué. It is a major Vietnamese landmark, each of its seven octagonal storeys symbolizing one of Buddha's reincarnations.

During the Vietnam war, it was an important centre of resistance. One of its monks, Thich Quang Duc, set fire to himself in Saigon in 1963, helping to precipitate the fall of the South Vietnamese government.

Thousands of islands are scattered across the transparent waters of Halong Bay. Top: The Bo Nau (Pelican) Grotto. Above and opposite: Junks are still used for fishing in the bay.

Halong Bay, stretching from the Red River Delta all the way up to the Chinese border, is one of the great natural wonders of Vietnam. Getting round it is a laborious process, since it involves countless ferries across the various branches of the Red River – although people always tell you there is a bridge about to be built. If this ever happens it will be a pity, because taking the ferry is an experience in its own right, and a great test of that Asian patience which foreigners would do well to acquire. The first rule in this part of the world is that the ferry you want is always on the wrong side of the river. But ferries are also an ideal place to meet ordinary people. In the space of a single journey, I shared a packet of cigarettes, bought a pastry from one vendor and declined the offer of a fistful of dried fish from another, and took a photo of a gang of children who elbowed one another out of the way to make sure they were in the viewfinder, pulling outlandish faces as they did so.

Finally, we arrived in Halong City, the ideal base for exploring this spectacular bay with its three thousand islands and shoreline as intricate as lace, shelving steeply into turquoise waters. The shapes

of the islands seem to change and move as banks of fog creep silently across the water. The locals like to describe the bay as the eighth wonder of the world and, although that is an exaggeration, the landscape does have a fairytale quality to it, for the water has worn away the limestone into the strange shapes typical of karst scenery.

Certainly the bay is to Vietnam what the Pyramids are to Egypt, and it would take weeks to do it full justice, since it is 1,200 square kilometres (480 square miles) in area and extends for hundreds of kilometres – as far as Quilin in China. I saw only a small part of it, the most spectacular, which involved a short boat trip from the small port of Bay Chal. I would like to have spent at least a day exploring the bay, perhaps continuing on to the port of Hong Gai, with its thriving coal and fishing industries.

The hundreds of rocks in the bay are known collectively in Vietnamese as *vinh ha long*, "the dragon which swims in the sea", the idea being that the rocks are the scales on its back.

The village of Hong Gai, in Halong Bay, is a popular starting point for boat trips and has one of the finest views of the bay. Coal from the nearby open-cast mines is exported from here, and Hong Gai is also a very busy fishing port.
Overleaf: This fishing junk in Halong Bay uses huge poles to extend its nets.

Halong Bay is an extraordinary maze of rocks, islands, inlets, and caves.

Each time we skirted a rock, we had another extraordinary view of this unforgettable landscape. The fishermen showed us rocks which (to those with a little imagination) were supposed to resemble a kneeling elephant, a bird taking flight, a buffalo on the back of a tortoise, and even a rather good caricature of General de Gaulle. Everything about Halong Bay fires the imagination, including the dozens of deep, mysterious caves. There is the Cave of Marvels, also known as the Cave of Wooden Stakes; the Drum Grotto, which makes a noise like a drumroll when the wind blows from the east; and Hong Han, a narrow underground passageway more than 2 kilometres (1 mile) long with a succession of immense caverns. The bay has also provided a hiding place for pirates since time immemorial, and many of the crews who ply between the islands have a swashbuckling air about them. But the fishermen themselves earn an honest living. The only act of piracy they commit is charging you several dollars to let you photograph their boats, with their reddish-brown dragon's-wing sails.

This area is full of tourists, and you have to choose the right angle

if you do not want the viewfinder to be filled with boatloads of Taiwanese visitors.

If you seek quiet and solitude, you will have to go a lot further away, past Surprise Island and Union Island and off into the unknown. The fishermen told me that some people who ventured that far never came back. Perhaps they had been seduced by a sea goddess or swallowed up by a dragon, or perhaps they simply got lost in the fog.

In the very near future, there will be a direct road from Hanoi to Halong City. New hotels are being built there already, and business is booming for vendors of tacky souvenirs. But the bay is big and beautiful enough to survive these incursions.

Before I left, I made a pilgrimage to the Halong 1 Hotel, which overlooks the bay from the side of a hill covered in bougainvillea, flame trees, and frangipani. The terrace restaurant of this beautifully maintained former colonial hotel has the finest sea view of any restaurant in Halong City.

We could have taken the helicopter to Hanoi if we had been in a hurry. The journey by road takes at least five hours, and is not exactly the epitome of comfort. But I preferred to see the Red River Delta from the ground rather than the air, despite the narrow roads and numerous ferry crossings. As always, I was constantly told that there would be a bridge soon.

In the villages along the way, I saw little black piglets rolling around in the dust and children tending the fruit trees. While I was waiting for the ferries (which, of course, were always on the wrong side of the river), I bought cans of drink and a green Vietcong hat. I even haggled over a bicycle, much to everyone's amusement. I would have been sorry to miss all this spontaneity and gentle kindness for the sake of saving a few hours by taking the helicopter.

I was all for heading straight to Hanoi, but Dong insisted that we stop off at a few pagodas. "They're on the way", he told me. "You won't regret it; they're really beautiful."

On the way? That turned out to be stretching the truth somewhat. We visited the Master's Pagoda, also known as the Heavenly Blessing

Pagoda, which is 40 kilometres (25 miles) south of the capital. We went to the Pagoda of the West and the Perfume Pagoda, both of them south-west of Hanoi. And we went to the Nin Phuc, Kiep Bac, and Keop Pagodas. I could not help feeling that we were going round in circles and Hanoi was not getting any nearer, but Dong kept insisting: "Come on, just one more!" Eventually, after this in-depth introduction to pagodas, there were no more left to see and we made our way to Hanoi, the capital.

This is northern Vietnam where, at first sight, everything seems more communist and austere than in the south. Even the European colonists' name for this part of the country, Tonkin, has a harsher, more military sound to it than the evocative name for southern Vietnam, Cochin-China. Hanoi does not yet have the go-getting brashness of its southern counterpart. It is a low-rise place, whereas Ho Chi Minh City seems intent on filling every tiny space with skyscrapers. Hanoi is the political capital; Ho Chi Minh City the financial capital. And of course it was Hanoi's forces that captured Saigon, as it then was.

Beautiful, exquisitely arranged bouquets of flowers are used as offerings to honour the dead and appease the gods.

Stallholders in the streets of Hanoi sell everything under the sun, from staples such as rice and fruit to luxuries such as porcelain and lottery tickets.

Hanoi has few of the millions of mopeds and motorcycles that pollute the air of Ho Chi Minh City. The relative quiet of its broad avenues is broken only by the incessant whirring hissing sound, characteristic of the city, of bicycles and *cyclos*, or cycle rickshaws. In some ways, it made more impression on me as a westerner than the constant din of Ho Chi Minh City. This was the tranquillity of a bygone age, and I was not used to the absence of engine noise and car horns. And there seemed to be hardly any lights on the night I arrived in Hanoi, as though the city were still at war and this were a blackout.

But it was dark simply because the city still has a very provincial dislike of neon signs, flashy shopfronts, and sodium street lamps.

There is nothing on earth quite like speeding through Hanoi in a *cyclo* at night, propelled through the dark streets and alleys by a set of flimsy bicycle wheels. By the standards of a car-driving westerner, the pace is positively snail-like, but it is still fast enough to be a white-knuckle experience rather than a leisurely amble with the wind in your hair. There were constant, sudden changes of direction, and the disorienting effect of the unlit roads made me completely lose track of my bearings. Suddenly, we were in downtown Hanoi. The journey did not take long, for the place feels more like a small town than a great capital city.

I got my first proper look at Hanoi early the next morning from Long Bien Bridge, which used to be named after the French governor-general, Paul Doumer. It was built across the Red River, linking the old town south of the river to the residential districts in the north-east, and was constantly bombed by the Americans during the war.

Each morning, tens of thousands of bicycles cross the bridge on

Above left and overleaf:
Ngoc Son (Jade Mountain) Temple
is reached by a little red wooden
bridge across Hoan Kiem Lake.

their way into and out of the city, passing on either side of the railway that runs along the middle. No other traffic is allowed. There are so many bicycles, and their speed is so constant, that the effect is of one river passing over another, and it would be suicidal to try to cross this great, unstoppable tide of often grotesquely overloaded boneshakers.

Even people's headwear was different here, with the greenish Vietcong hat replacing the cones of rice-straw and small, elegant organdie hats worn by women in the south. Below the bridge, a group of fishermen mended their boats beside the dark brown waters of the Red River, an old woman steered a herd of ducks along the riverbank, and half-naked children played on the deck of a barge.

Of course, there is another more modern bridge, the Chuong Duong Bridge, which cars and lorries are allowed to use. Hanoi is not just an open-air museum; it is also a major capital, with suburbs radiating out from the historic city centre.

For several years now, there has been conflict between those whose first concern is to preserve the city's charm, and those who want to turn it into a modern metropolis.

This is a touchy subject with some people. My young guide in Hanoi, Vu Van Khang (whose name means "success and prosperity"), was a strong advocate of progress. "We're trying to move away from being a third-world country. Why try to stop us? I'm sure you find it all very picturesque, all these outdoor restaurants with people cooking noodles in the street, and the *cyclos*, and the crumbling buildings with corrugated-iron roofs, but surely the Vietnamese people are entitled to have taxis, hygienic restaurants, modern buildings with lifts and air conditioning, and department stores like those in London or Hong Kong?" But the city council is

Opposite: The One Pillar Pagoda was built by Emperor Ly Thai Tong in the eleventh century as a mark of thanks to Quan The Am Bo Tat, the goddess of mercy, for having given him a son. Since the goddess is always depicted seated on a lotus flower, the pagoda itself is lotus-shaped, built on a single pillar in the water.
Above: The Temple of Literature (Van Mieu) also dates from the eleventh century. It was Vietnam's first university, built for the sons of princes and mandarins.

A former pagoda converted into a café in Hanoi.

sticking to its guns. It has just refused planning permission for an eight-storey hotel near the Little Lake, and intends to build a new city outside the old town and the colonial district.

If this project does come to fruition, it would strike a balance between preserving the past and building for the future – a kind of compromise – unlikely to happen in any other Asian country. I hoped that Hanoi would not be ruined in the same way as Bangkok, Beijing, and Shanghai, but things are complicated by the fact that there are many aspects of Vietnam's past that people would rather forget. They do not want to be reminded of the colonial era. "We're a young nation, but we're fifty years behind the times", Vu Van Khang told me. "We've got a lot of catching up to do. You Europeans come from old countries and you venerate the past. The older a church is, the more valuable it is in your eyes. But that's not a concept that we young Vietnamese understand."

I heard the opposite point of view while I was strolling round the Temple of Literature. Tran Thi Lan ("fertile orchid") was an art student who had come to make some sketches of the building. "I'm

18, so I missed the war, but I know we need to preserve our roots. The Vietnamese people have been shaped by history. If we burn our boats, we'll become like the rest of the world, with no soul. I think perhaps we need to become more affluent, or at least a little less poor, and I hope we do, but we must remain Vietnamese and hold on to our religious, literary, and architectural heritage, even if it's been imposed on us by others, like the colonial administrators' quarter."

The colonial district is another subject that polarizes people. Some would raze it to the ground overnight, given half a chance, while others would rather leave it as it stands, even at the risk of being

Quan Than Pagoda, also known as Tran Vo Temple, sits on the edge of the delightful little lake of Truc Bach. Its altars are dedicated to Chinese divinities, and it also has a statue of Confucius.

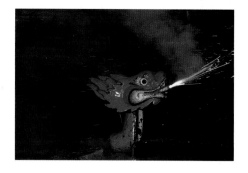

accused of neo-colonialist attitudes. Personally, I thought it was beautiful, with its wide, French-style streets and avenues, centuries-old trees, and broad pavements.

I particularly liked its houses, which look like middle-class turn-of-the-century French seaside homes transported to the depths of Indochina. Were it not for the climate, I could almost imagine myself to be somewhere like Deauville, and the style of these attractive patrician houses has indeed been dubbed "Normandy pagoda". The French quarter is probably safe from the bulldozers, since the people who live there tend to be influential senior party officials.

I could have toured Hanoi on foot or in a *cyclo*, but I decided to go by bike because it was such a good way of meeting Vietnamese people. I abandoned my attempts to buy one, and rented one instead. The city centre has hardly changed for half a century, particularly the old town, or "City of the Thirty-Six Streets", which is divided into districts, each occupied by a particular craft or trade. There is the famous Hung Dao (Silk) Street, and other streets are devoted to cotton, copper, poultry, hemp, and even playing cards.

In Hanoi's famous water-puppet shows, the puppets dance a surreal aquatic ballet.

In this maze of narrow thoroughfares, dating back to the fifteenth century, you can find anything if you look hard: Russian watches, silk scarves, round hats, pointed hats, Vietcong caps, old French street signs, paper flowers and pagodas, tin-plate toys, embroidered tablecloths, ceramics, antique compasses, opium pipes and weights for weighing opium shaped like elephants, phoenixes and pagodas, silver jewellery, leather sandals, fake Ray Bans, and the inevitable counterfeit T-shirts and polo shirts bearing leading international brand names. Here, everything can be bought or sold for a matter of a few dollars.

Boats slip noiselessly through the rice fields at Hoa Lu, at the southern end of the Red River Delta, 120 kilometres (75 miles) from Hanoi. This is the site of the ancient capital of the Dinh dynasty.

Feeling peckish? You'll find excellent French-style baguettes in Hanoi, with French sausage and cheese to go with them. I sat down, or rather squatted, at an open-air restaurant on a tiny three-legged wooden stool, and ate clear noodles from an enamel dish.

I finished this banquet with an ice cream on the "lovers' promenade" beside Truc Bach Lake. By this time, I had realized that the city and its lifestyle was a lot more laid-back and friendly than its austere appearance suggested, and the old imperial city had retained much of its beauty. Truc Bach Lake is surrounded by flame trees. Beside it is the thousand-year-old Tran Vo Pagoda, named after the god of the north, whose symbols were the snake and the tortoise. I wandered round Hoan Kiem Lake, or the Lake of the Restored Sword, with the diminutive Tortoise Pagoda set on an islet in the middle of the water. The banks also serve as an open-air gymnasium, and local people come here at the crack of dawn to practise their ancient, slow-motion gymnastics. I also went to West Lake, or Big Lake, which was once surrounded by palaces. All that remains today is the fine pagoda of Tran Quoc, whose garden is an ideal place to sit, rest, and enjoy the peace and quiet while it lasts.

You are never very far away from a temple or pagoda in Hanoi. There is the delicate One Pillar Pagoda, made entirely of wood and resting on a single stone pillar in a lotus-covered pond. Elsewhere, the Temple of Literature or Writers' Pagoda is dedicated to Confucius, and was Vietnam's first faculty of letters, in the eleventh century. The Jade Mountain Temple is on another island in Hoan Kiem Lake, and is reached by a red lacquered bridge. The Ambassadors' Pagoda is the centre of Buddhism in the city, and was used to accommodate foreign emissaries in the sixteenth century. The Trung Sisters' Pagoda is dedicated to the queens of Tonkin who, two thousand years ago, died rather than submit to the Chinese. But Hanoi also has another "temple": Ho Chi Minh's Mausoleum, which forms part of every organized tour. My main memory of it is not the beauty of its architecture, which is based on a lotus-flower motif, but the emotion it evoked among my fellow visitors.

Above and opposite: A boat trip takes you to the temple of the Le and Dinh dynasties at Hoa Lu. The emperors are guarded by stone dragons.

Foreign tourists are given priority, but I was moved by the long queues of peasants, village schoolchildren, old women, and young couples making the pilgrimage here. Their heads were bare under the broiling sun, and their arms dangled by their sides because they were not allowed to wear hats or put their hands in their pockets. They waited hours for the privilege of paying a few seconds' silent homage to the mummified body of the man who liberated their country from French rule. I went on to inspect Ho Chi Minh's house, set amid tranquil and imposing grounds. Bizarre though the visit may have been, it helped me to gain a better understanding of this country and its contradictions. Capitalism may have won the upper hand as far as the economy is concerned, but communist ideology still dominates the everyday lives of the Vietnamese people.

I was also curious to know more about the revolution, or at least the official view of it, so I went to the Army Museum, with its collection of crashed aircraft, racks of bombs, and models of major battles. I went on to the Fine Arts Museum, where contemporary revolutionary art predominates on all but the first floor.

I found that the Ho Chi Minh Museum, the Revolutionary Museum, and the Independence Museum were all in a similarly propagandistic vein. Only in the History Museum was I able to discover some of the reality of ancient Vietnam, but even here a large part of the final section was devoted to the war of liberation.

I ended the day with one of Hanoi's most popular entertainments: a water-puppet performance on the shores of Hoan Kiem Lake, with the figurines seemingly dancing a ballet on the water's surface.

*W*orking in the rice fields, in Ha Son Binh province, south-west of Hanoi.
Planting out rice is a painstaking task as each plant has to be handled individually.
Overleaf: Ploughing terraced rice paddies in Cao Cai province.

• Tribal music and dance •

The Vietnamese refer to the people of the mountains as the Moi, a term best avoided when talking to them, since it means "savages". Each ethnic group has its own musical tradition, some influenced by Vietnamese music, but all quite distinctive and often deeply moving.

The most common instruments are various kinds of flutes, recorders, bamboo instruments resembling bagpipes, xylophone-like percussion instruments, gongs, and drums. Some of the dances are for women only, and others for men. Most are laden with symbolism.

That evening, Dong announced that we were off on a five-day trip to the far north of Vietnam, to explore the region south of the Chinese border and east of Laos.

This was something of a major expedition, since in the north the highways marked so confidently on the map often bear little resemblance to roads. Some of them were little short of dreadful, but it was an unforgettable journey nevertheless.

It took us two days just to cover the 450 kilometres (280 miles) from Hanoi to Dien Bien Phu, stopping off at Son La along the way. We could have done the trip with Vietnam Airlines or in army helicopters, but that would have meant missing out on a spectacular mountain landscape and on meeting the montagnard tribes in a region which, until recently, was closed to foreign visitors. The road climbed gently up through the valleys as the mountains rose more and more steeply on either side. Soon, the asphalt had given out, which in some ways was an improvement because it meant that the potholes were less deep.

All the same, our military jeep had a tough time negotiating the

rocks, mud-filled holes, and streams that littered the road. Here and there we saw groups of women mending it with shovels and huge heaps of earth and stone, but it was a Sisyphean task; they were simply patching up the damage done by the last rainstorm before the next one undid half the work they had done. In some of the larger villages, there were bright yellow excavators lined up on the verge. Soon, we were promised, there would be a proper road. We turned a corner and saw a cluster of houses in front of us. Dong suggested that we stop for a while. This was the country of the Dao people, and the wooden village seemed to have been built over a series of bumps and holes. "Those are bomb craters", Dong told me nonchalantly. He pointed out the semicircular steel drinking-troughs that people had placed outside their houses for the pigs: on closer examination, these proved to have been made from bombs picked up by the villagers.

Dozens of tribes inhabit this tranquil region: Nung, Man, Tho, Black Tai, White Tai, Muong, Hmong. The central and provincial governments are trying to persuade them to move to the valleys, but

Opposite, top: Wild, or mountain rice, being grown at Lai Chan in the northern plateaux. This has a lower yield than ordinary rice grown in paddy fields and gives only one crop a year, but fetches much higher prices.

Opposite, bottom: A M'nong woman picks her way across the fragile earth levees that separate the terraced rice paddies.

Above: Women from the Red Zao tribe at Lai Cheu market in northern Vietnam.

*P*eople of the Flowery Hmong tribe harvesting wild rice.
Everyone in the village, children included, is expected to help out.
Opposite: A girl from the Dao Khoa tribe.

• Minority peoples •

According to the last official census, there were around sixty ethnic minority groups in the high plains of the centre and the south and the mountains of the north. The French colonialists called them montagnards, and they have settled there over centuries, if not millennia, often being pushed further into the hills by new arrivals. They belong to three main groups: Khmer; Tai and Lao; and Chinese, with successive waves of people coming from places as far away as Tibet and Mongolia. These groups – the Hmong, Mien, Cham, M'nong and Tay to mention only the largest – are animists. They often live in villages on stilts, and the women wear very varied and brightly coloured traditional costumes. Many of the groups have surprisingly distinctive musical cultures.

A Hmong boy and his dog, in a house on stilts in the small village of Moc Chau.

they prefer to live in the mountains to which they moved as the people of the plains advanced, and they still practise extensive rice culture using slash-and-burn techniques.

Others raise cattle, pigs, and goats, and most have retained their traditional lifestyles and costumes.

The little town of Dien Bien Phu is close to the border with Laos, and has a population of ten thousand. It looks peaceful enough, and it is difficult to imagine that this was the site of the great battle in 1954 that marked the end of the French presence in Indochina. Here, French troops were placed under a lengthy siege by the Vietminh, and were eventually defeated. There are many reminders of this historic event in and around the town: the French commander's headquarters, which have been restored; some trenches; the rusting remains of military equipment; and memorials to the thousands of Vietnamese and French fighters who died. All this seems distant and unreal in this peaceful valley surrounded by tree-covered mountains. The tall grass and bushes have regrown, and new trees have been planted.

*A*bove right and top: Women from the Zao ethnic minority making sheaves of rice-straw, which are then laid out to dry in the courtyard or village square.
Left: Woman from the Nung minority.

Vietnamese life is dominated by religion and Communism in equal measure. The North Vietnamese government tried to gain control over the various faiths, but they are now re-emerging on a grand scale. Caodaism has over two million adherents, and more than 10% of the population is Christian, making Vietnam the leading Christian country in Asia after the Philippines. The influence of Islam is marginal – there are only around 5,000 believers. But the traditional religions of Buddhism, Confucianism, and Taoism, all of them combined to a greater or lesser extent with the animist practices and geomancy common throughout the region, play a significant part in the lives of most Vietnamese people.

CONFUCIANISM

Confucianism is more of a way of life than a religion. It was developed in China in the sixth century BC by Confucius, or Khong Tu, and introduced to Vietnam in the second century AD. Confucianists believe that man is shaped by his culture and by his position in the community, but through study can improve both himself and society.

Confucianists have therefore developed a complex system of learning, designed to allow individuals to build on their knowledge and to gain in virtue, since only acquired virtues, not accidents of birth, allow people to assume leading roles in society. This philosophy therefore places the emphasis on individual duty to society and the family, and on worshipping one's ancestors. The danger of this world view is that it can result in an unwillingness to change, and this has been a particular problem in Vietnam ever since the fifteenth century.

TAOISM

Taoism, based on the philosophy of Lao Tzu, grew up in China in about the sixth century BC. It did not become a religion until the second century AD. This complex vision of the world centres on contemplation and the quest for simplicity, which ultimately leads to Tao, the absolute, eternal reality. It has been influenced by many outside factors, including Buddhism, and involves the worship of a series of gods representing the forces of nature. This has gradually evolved into spirit and demon worship.

This page and opposite: The annual pilgrimage to the Perfume Pagoda, 60 kilometres (37 miles) south-west of Hanoi.
The pilgrimage takes place between the middle of the second lunar month and the last week of the third lunar month, and attracts considerable crowds.
Overleaf: Boatmen and women awaiting the return of pilgrims from the Perfume Pagoda.

VIETNAMESE BUDDHISM

The Buddhism practised in Vietnam is a synthesis of the Chinese Buddhist tradition of Mahayana, meaning the "greater vehicle", and the Indian doctrine of Theravada, or "lesser vehicle". Theravada Buddhism aspires towards withdrawal from the world and towards Nirvana, while Mahayana believes in developing human virtues and teaching by example. In everyday life, both have been greatly influenced by animism and polytheism, and also by the Taoists' belief in universal divine forces and the Confucians' striving for virtue. Most importantly, Vietnamese Buddhists also practise ancestor worship.

RELIGIOUS CEREMONIES

This overlap between religions means that nearly all Vietnamese people take part in fairly similar ceremonies, regardless of what religious tradition they belong to, which can be quite confusing for a foreigner. These ceremonies, whether Taoist, Confucianist, or Buddhist, are essentially based on a belief in omnipresent spirits.

In addition, Caodaism, which is practised by a fifth of the population, actually makes a virtue of its eclectic nature and the way in which it borrows elements from other religions.

The Vietnamese give expression to their faith in three main ceremonies: *Khan, Cung,* and *Te. Khan* is a very personal form of prayer, while *Cung* is a ceremony in which an individual, family, or group makes an offering to the spirits. Depending on which religion the people belong to, this may consist of flowers, fruit, meat, or glutinous rice; incense is nearly always used for purification. *Te* is a solemn ceremony held in honour of the most important spirits on special occasions such as pilgrimages to the Perfume Pagoda, and also incorporates the other two forms of ceremony involving individual prayer at the altar and offerings to the spirits.

The Perfume Pagoda is a collection of Buddhist temples on the slopes of Huong Tich Mountain, the Mountain of the Fragrant Traces. The easiest way of getting there is by boat. Opposite: Pilgrims lighting incense sticks outside Thap Huong Temple. This page, top: Thap Huong Temple. Above left: Making an offering to a stone statue of a lion. Above right: The steps leading to the sacred grotto of Huong Tich Chu, or the Pagoda of the Perfumed Vestige.

The gods in the Pagoda leading to Heaven (above) and the Purgatorial Pagoda (opposite) purify the souls of pilgrims who visit them. There is also a thriving trade in religious souvenirs.

On my last day, Dong came with me to Hanoi Airport. He was returning to Ho Chi Minh City, but he could not afford to fly, and so was taking the two-day train journey instead. I was departing for a completely different world, and by the time Paris hove into sight, he was still somewhere near Hué. I was immensely grateful to him for having patiently accompanied me the length and breadth of his country for nearly a month, and for having gone to so much effort to ensure that I saw some of the hidden facets of Vietnam. He was a likeable and erudite guide, and his parting words were: "Thank you for coming … Please make sure you tell your friends to come too!"

USEFUL INFORMATION

INFORMATION BUREAUX: Vietnam has no tourist agencies in the
UK. However, you can obtain basic information and a map of
Vietnam from the Vietnamese Embassy. In Vietnam itself further
information is available from the Commercial and Tourist
Service Centre, 1 Ba Frien, Hanoi, tel. 00844-8265244,
fax 00844-8256418.

TRAVEL AGENCIES IN VIETNAM: The National Tourism Bureau has
a network of tourist information offices in Vietnam, called
Vietnam Tourism (Du Lich Viet Nam), 69-71 Nam Ky Khoi
Nghia, D3, Ho Chi Minh City, tel. 00848-829127, fax 00848-
8224987. Other state travel agencies are Saigon Tourist and
Hanoi Tourism: Saigon Tourist, 49 Le Thanh Ton, Ho Chi Minh
City, tel. 00848-8230102, fax 00848-8224987; Hanoi Tourism,
18 Ly Thuong Kiet, Hanoi, tel. 00844-8266714,
fax 00844-8254209. Tours are now also available from
other semi-state and private sector travel agencies.

ENTRY FORMALITIES: You need a valid passport and a
visa to enter Vietnam. Visas can be obtained direct
from the Vietnamese embassies or through your
travel agent. To get a visa you will require a valid
passport and two passport photographs, and
there will be a fee. It usually takes seven to ten
days for a tourist visa to come through, but it
is best to allow four weeks. A visa remains valid
for a month.

VIETNAMESE EMBASSY: Embassy of the Socialist Republic of Vietnam, 12-14 Victoria Road, London W8 5RD; tel. 0171 937 1912; fax 0171 938 4625.

BRITISH EMBASSY IN VIETNAM: 16 Ly Thuong Kiet Street, Hanoi; tel. +84 48 252349; fax +84 48 265762.

HEALTH AND INOCULATIONS: Inoculations are not compulsory unless you are entering the country from an area where yellow fever is prevalent. However, inoculations against hepatitis (A and B), Japanese encephalitis, tetanus, polio and typhus are recommended. Malaria is widespread in Vietnam. Mosquito netting and anti-mosquito spray or cream are therefore essential. It is also advisable to wear long sleeves and long trousers in the evening. Opinion is divided over prophylactic treatment against malaria; it is a good idea to consult your doctor or a specialist in tropical medicine before you travel.

MONEY AND FOREIGN CURRENCY: The Vietnamese unit of currency is the dong (pronounced *doum*). The exchange rate in April 1997 was 11,500 dong to one US dollar. On entering Vietnam you must declare any foreign currency above the sum of $2000. US dollars are widely accepted, and you should have a good supply of $1 or $5 bills with you. It is also a good idea to have a few dong ready to hand, for visiting museums, buying stamps or conducting any other transactions for less than a dollar. European currencies can be changed at banks. The big hotels and travel agencies also accept the following credit cards: Visa, Eurocard, Mastercard, Eripluscard, Diners Club.

CUSTOMS REGULATIONS: On entering the country you will be given two customs forms and an entry form to fill in. Keep one of the customs forms and the entry form until you leave. Vietnamese currency must not be taken out of the country.

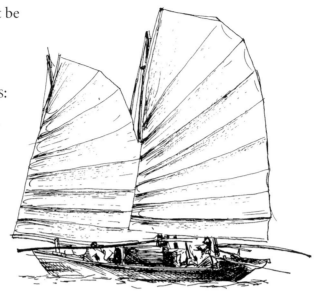

GETTING TO VIETNAM – AIRLINES: Vietnam is reached by air with a stopover in Bangkok or Hongkong. Many European airlines stop over in European cities as well. International airlines operating flights to Hanoi and Ho Chi Minh City (Saigon) include: Vietnam Airlines, Air France, Air UK, British Midland, China Airlines, Malaysia Airlines, Swissair, Thai Airways International and Transavia Airlines. The total journey time from London Heathrow or Gatwick is 16 to 17 hours. The peak season for flights to Vietnam is between 15 December and 25 January, the time of the Tet new year festival. After that season prices are considerably lower. Ideally, if you wish to visit both north and south Vietnam, choose flights that will allow you to arrive in Ho Chi Minh City and leave from Hanoi or vice versa.

The Country and the People

GEOGRAPHY: Vietnam is north of the equator, between the 8th parallel and the northern tropic, about 10,000 km (6,200 miles) from Britain. From north to south it stretches over a distance of 1,600 kilometres (1,000 miles), while from east to west it is between 60 and 600 kilometres (37-370 miles) wide. More than three-quarters of the country consists of hills, high plateaux and mountains. Vietnam has narrow coastal plains in the middle, and two broad alluvial plains, created by the Red River (Song Hong) and the Mekong, in the north and south. The Vietnamese northern border is with China, the central border with Laos, and the southern border with Cambodia.

AREA: With a surface area of 329, 559 km² (127,212 square miles) Vietnam is slightly larger than the UK and Ireland.

CAPITAL: Hanoi, with a population of 3 million. However, the business centre of the country is Ho Chi Minh City (Saigon), with a population of 5 million people.

FORM OF GOVERNMENT: A Socialist Republic since 1976. The head of state is Tran Nuc Luong (President since September 1997).

ECONOMY: Among the major products are rice, rubber, foodstuffs, textiles, cement and chemicals. Fishing is also an important source of revenue. The main industry is the shipping of crude oil. Other industries: the cultivation of sugar cane, maize, cotton, tea, coffee and tobacco; silkworm rearing, livestock breeding, forest exploitation and fisheries.

CLIMATE: Stretching, as it does a thousand miles from north to south, Vietnam spans several different climatic zones. The north is sub-tropical, with hot, humid summers and mild winters. Average temperatures in Hanoi are 17°C (63°F) in January and 29°C (84°F) in July. The Pass of Clouds in the centre of the country represents a meteorological divide. South of the pass the climate is hot and tropical at all times of the year, with average temperatures of 25 to 30°C (77 to 86°F). In Saigon light clothing is worn all the year round. You will need warmer clothing for the north and centre of Vietnam in winter (Hué, Da Nang, Da Lat). The rainy season is from May to September. There are frequent typhoons in August and September. No one season is best for travelling to Vietnam as a whole; it all depends where you are going. The sea temperature is a constant 24 to 28°C (75 to 82°F).

LOCAL TIME: GMT + 7 hours.

POPULATION: About 75 million, half of them under the age of 20. The Vietnamese call themselves *Kinh*, dwellers in the plains. Today north and south Vietnamese are a mixed race, both physically and in terms of lifestyle. 13% of the people belong to one or other of the 54 minorities such as the Muong, Tay and Thai, Mon-Khmer and Meo-Dao. There are over a million Chinese, called *Hoa*, live in Vietnam.

RELIGION: Most Vietnamese believe in the spiritual powers of nature (animism). The Primeval Mother Au Co (the mountain goddess) and the Primeval Father Lac Long (the dragon king) head the pantheon of natural divinities, together with the mountain spirit Than Nui and the water spirit

Than Thuy. In ancestor worship, the souls of the dead are honoured at the domestic altar for three generations, keeping them alive and present in the memory. Other widely practised religions are Taoism, Confucianism and Buddhism, which have merged together under Chinese and local animist influence to form the Tam Gioa (threefold religion). There are small religious minorities of Christians, Muslims and Hindus.

LANGUAGE: Vietnamese, spoken with different local accents, is the national language. Minorities also speak Chinese and various Mon Khmer and Malaysian-Polynesian dialects. The language is complex, and is written using the Roman alphabet. Accents denote pitch and syllabic emphasis. Depending on the accent, the same word may mean completely different things. For instance, the syllable *ma* can mean "spirit", "mother", "rice germ", "ditch" or "horse".

The main foreign language is English, spoken by young people in particular. Older people often speak French, a legacy from the colonial past. A number of people also speak Russian and German, since many Vietnamese once lived in former East Germany.

TOURIST ATTRACTIONS:

There are many beautiful sights in Vietnam. On no account should you miss seeing the following:

The breathtaking BAY OF HALONG, which lies east of Hanoi in the north of the country, and contains countless close-packed, curiously shaped limestone islands and grottos. You can take a round trip from HONG GAI and see some of the grottos, for instance the BO-NAU CAVE (pelican cave) and the HANG-HANH TUNNEL, which is almost 2 kilometres (1 ¼ miles) long. The most spectacular grotto is the HANG DAU GO (grotto of wonders), which is full of stalagmites and stalactites reminiscent of human and animal figures. In HANOI itself, the eleventh-century Old Town is well worth seeing. Each of its many streets and alleys is named after the product sold there. The TRAN QUOC PAGODA should not be missed either. This sixth-century Buddhist temple lies on the south-east bank of the Western Lake. The former harbour town of Hoi An, with its traditional Chinese houses, lies in the central region, 22 kilometres (14 miles) from the Marble Mountains. From here you can go upstream along the THU BON by boat to the rapids just before MY SON. This temple city is the largest complex to have been preserved from the imperial Champa period. The imperial city of HUÉ and the grave of KING TU DUC are in the same area. Going further south, you reach the MEKONG DELTA, the third largest river delta in the world after those of the Amazon and the Brahmaputra. It is the rice-basket of the nation, but many exotic fruits also grow well there, including lychees, mangoes and papayas, and so do soya beans, tobacco and sugar cane. Do not miss seeing one of the many floating markets, for instance the market in PHUNG HIEP, or those in the CHOLON CHINESE quarter of Ho Chi Minh City, which in itself has nothing very notable worth seeing. The GIAC-LAM PAGODA is thought to be the city's oldest, dating from 1744, and has remained relatively unchanged. The BEN-THAN MARKET, an indoor market built by the French, is an attractive sight.

INTERNAL TRANSPORT: Internal air transport in Vietnam is good; the planes are quite new and there is a computerized reservations system. Flights are relatively inexpensive. Trains in Vietnam are

Vietnam are very slow, going at little more than 55 kph (34 mph). They are not very comfortable either, and are often booked out. You need to reserve a seat several days in advance. If you want to explore the country by car you will have to hire a chauffeur-driven vehicle. Air conditioning will cost extra, and you should find out in advance whether the driver's accommodation and food are included in the price. There is an extensive bus network in Vietnam, with express buses travelling certain routes, and minibuses especially for tourists. You will find bicycle rickshaws and inexpensive taxis in all the cities.

VIETNAMESE CUISINE: Vietnamese cuisine has been subject to many different influences. China and the adjoining areas, as well as France, have all made their culinary mark. The dishes available from the stalls to be found in every market and along the streets are simple, inexpensive and tasty. These stalls usually offer only one dish, either a stir-fry, freshly prepared in a wok, or a soup with strips of meat and very fresh vegetables. The many different varieties of rice are often served with *nuoc mam* (a transparent-looking fish sauce) or *nuoc cham*, a sauce made from garlic, chili, sugar and fresh lemon juice.

Although all information was carefully checked at the time of going to press (November 1997), the publisher cannot accept any responsibility for its accuracy.

Philippe BODY: pages 8-9, 11, 16, 18, 19, 20, 21, 22, 24-25, 27 top right, 28-29, 30, 31, 32, 33, 34, 36-37, 38, 39, 40, 41, 42-43, 44, 45, 46, 60 top, 61, 62, 63 right, 66 bottom, 67, 68-69, 70, 71, 73 top, 74-75, 76, 78 bottom, 79, 80-81, 82, 83 top, 84, 86, 87 top, 91, 92, 96 top, 97, 98-99, 100 top, 101, 103 top, 106, 122, 148-149.

Jean-Léo DUGAST: pages 12, 13, 14-15, 26, 27 left, 47, 48, 49, 50-51, 52, 53, 54, 55, 56, 57, 58-59, 64-65, 66 top, 77, 83 bottom, 89, 93, 94-95, 96 bottom, 103 bottom, 114, 118, 119, 121 bottom, 127, 128, 129, 130, 134 top, 135, 136, 138, 139, 140 top, 146.

Alain EVRARD: page 107.

Olivier MARTEL: pages 132-133.

Luc NGAN: page 85.

Philippe NOIROT: pages 23, 35, 73 bottom, 104 bottom, 116, 117, 120.

Jean PAOLI: pages 102, 103 right, 104 top, 108-109, 113, 115, 121 top.

Michel RENAUDEAU: pages 87 bottom, 96 left, 100 bottom, 105, 110, 111, 112, 121 bottom.

Philippe RENAULT: page 17.

Hubert RUIZ: pages 63 top, 72, 78 top, 90.

Emmanuel VALENTIN: page 60 bottom.

Xavier ZIMBARDO: pages 134 left, 137.